TWO PEAS IN A POUCH

'A Diary of Two Orphaned Joeys ~ Book 1'

Sagey Boi" Boi" & Bluebelle

First published by Ultimate World Publishing 2024
Copyright © 2024 Ingrid L Kangas

ISBN

Paperback: 978-1-923255-67-8
Ebook: 978-1-923255-68-5

Ingrid L Kangas has asserted her rights under the Copyright, Designs and Patents Act 1988 to be identified as the Author and Illustrator of this work. The information in this book is based on the author's experiences and opinions. The publisher specifically disclaims responsibility for any adverse consequences which may result from use of the information contained herein. Permission to use information has been sought by the author. Any breaches will be rectified in further editions of the book.

All rights reserved. No part of this publication may be reproduced, stored in or introduced into a retrieval system, or transmitted in any form, or by any means (electronic, mechanical, photocopying, recording or otherwise) without the prior written permission of the author. Any person who does any unauthorised act in relation to this publication may be liable to criminal prosecution and civil claims for damages. Enquiries should be made through the publisher.

Cover design: Ultimate World Publishing,
Illustrations: Ingrid L Kangas
Layout and typesetting: Ultimate World Publishing
Editor: Victoria Pickens
Heart to the Sea Photography By Jade Barclay
1 x photo of Author-Illustrator back of book

Ultimate World Publishing
Diamond Creek,
Victoria Australia 3089
www.writeabook.com.au

Dedication

~ Dear Mum & Dad,

~ My grown kiddies, Dale, Timmy, Naomi & Johnny,

Also ~ Tamika, Alexei & Rachel, may this inspire you to follow your heart's desire, it's never too late.

"Jag Alskar Dig"

~ Bluebelle, Sagey Boi Boi

All Mumma, Papa & Bubba Roos,

I am grateful for all you continue to teach & remind me,

of what is truly important,

~ Love, kindness, understanding, support, respect

~ Listen to your heart

~ Look and see

~ Nature is whispering messages

~ Will You Care ?

In Loving Kindness
Ingrid Lorraine Kangas

*I would like to acknowledge the
Traditional Owners and Custodians of this land,
The Yuin (Djuwin) People here on the South Coast
NSW, on which we creatively work and live,
with its diverse bushlands, sea, wildlife and nature,
I pay my respects to Elders, past, present and
emerging.*

Note to Reader~Storybook Lovers

~ This book can be read in two different sittings, being a two chapter book, like ~ two story books in ~ 1

Look 'n Find Me ( )~ I am hiding in every illustration, in different colours, on this fun journey

with **Bluebelle** & **Sagey Boi ' Boi '**

www.snugglepouchstudios.com

Chapter ~ 1

'Snug 'n Sweet'

There's a Story ... that needs to be told

Of how 2 Peas in a pouch ... unfolds,

Not the Peas that are Green,

Small and Sweet.

These Lil' Treats have Bounceeey ~ Feet.

When Bluebelle and Sagey were tiny

little Joeys,

Hiding down in a pouch snug

... yet not sure.

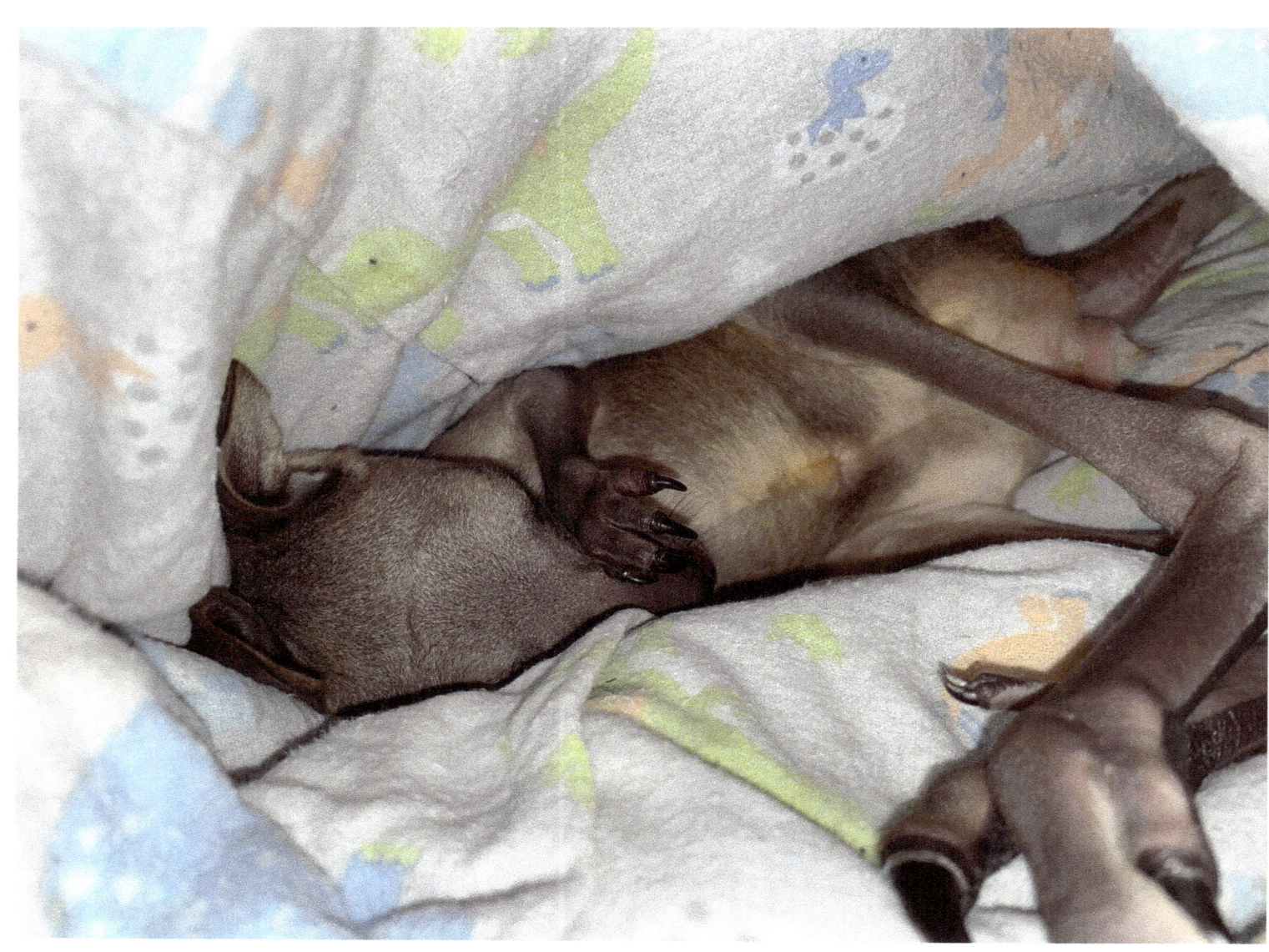

A MADE pouch ... is

sooooooooooooooooooo different,

from the Warm ... Sticky

Oily one ... Mother had held onto

Us before.

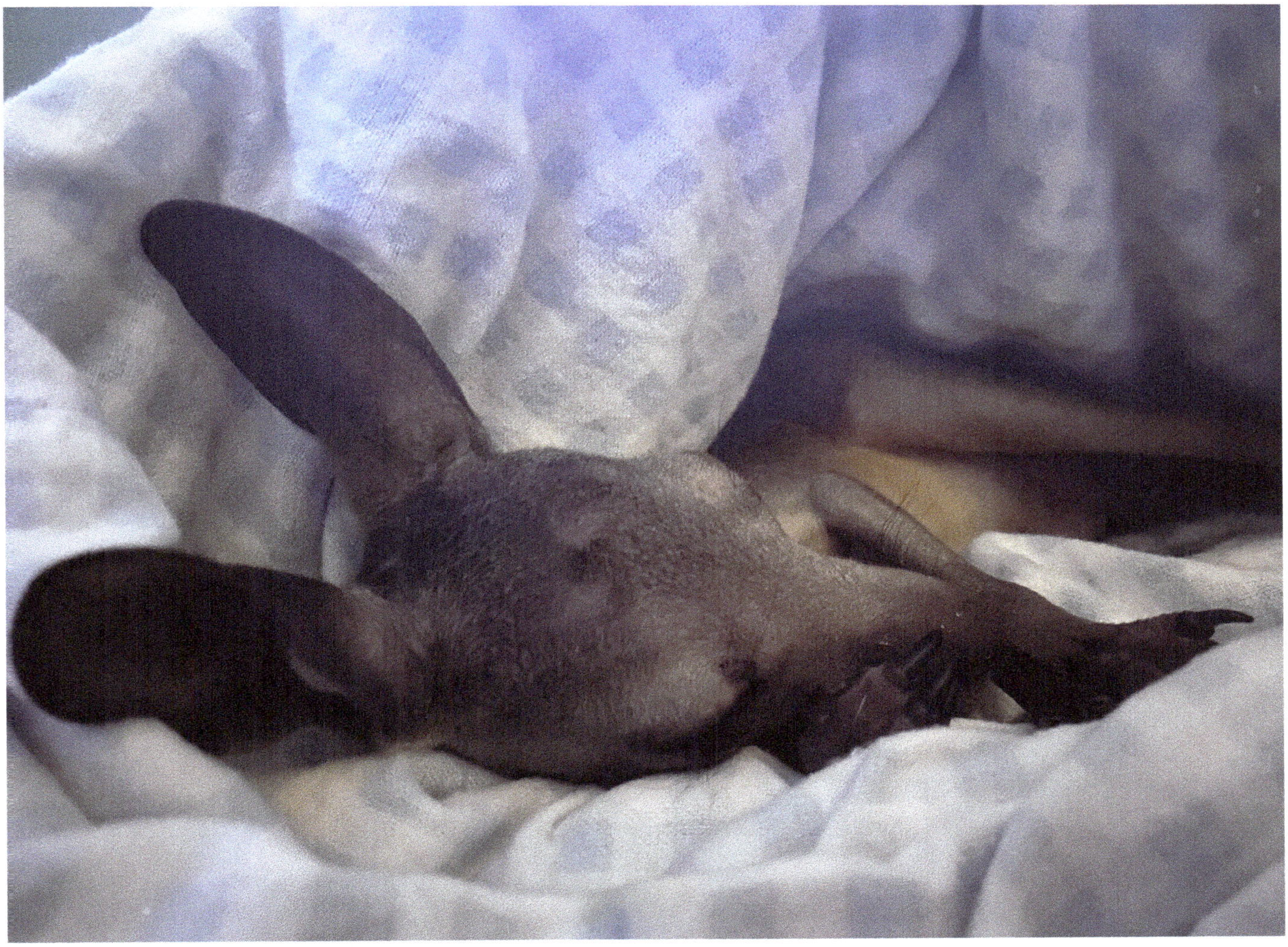

After many days ... weeks passing

with quiet ... Loving care,

Little faces ... Big ... Eyes open

keen to appear,

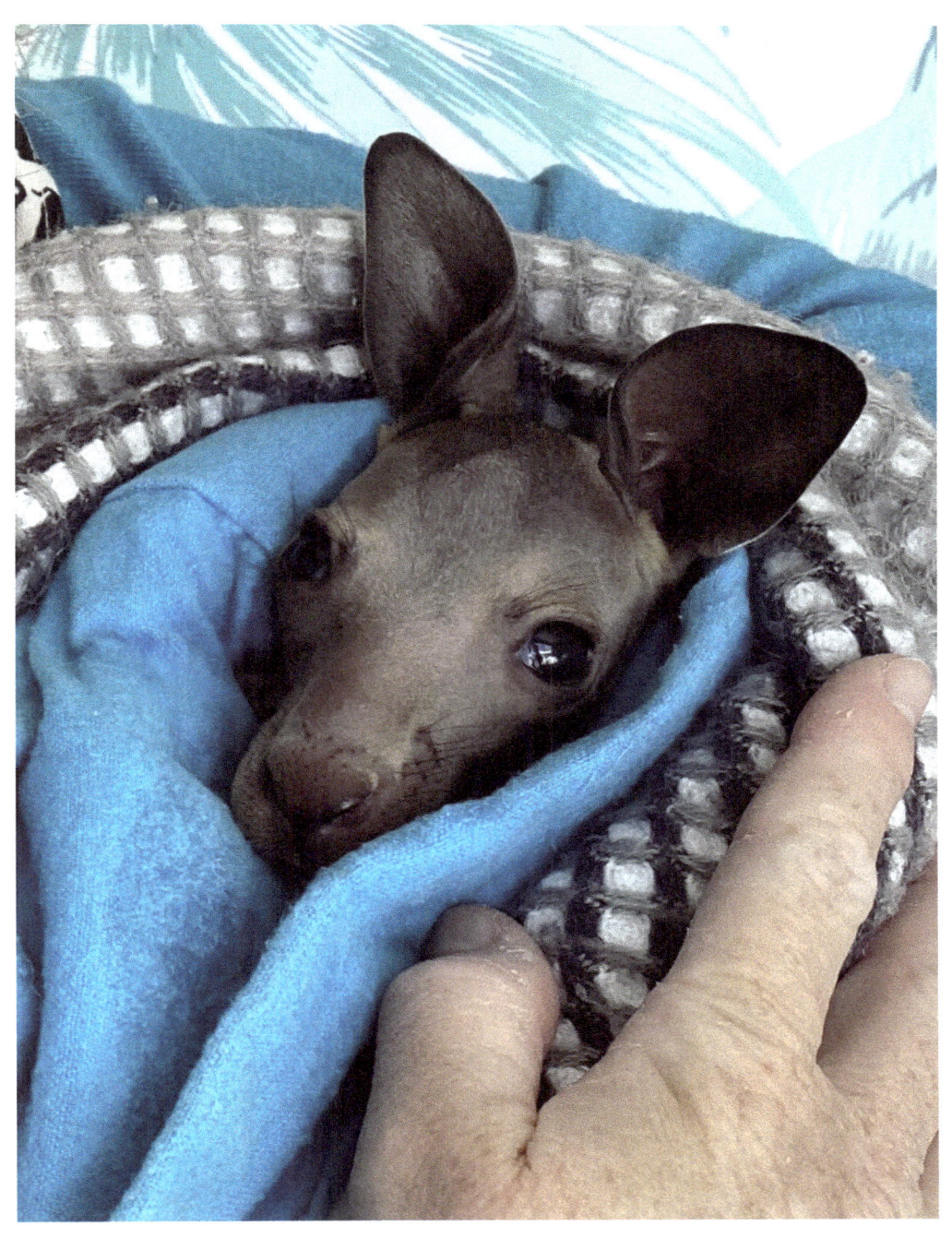

More often for warm bottles ...
gentle face stroke 'n clean,

Helping them adjust 'n feel

Dear.

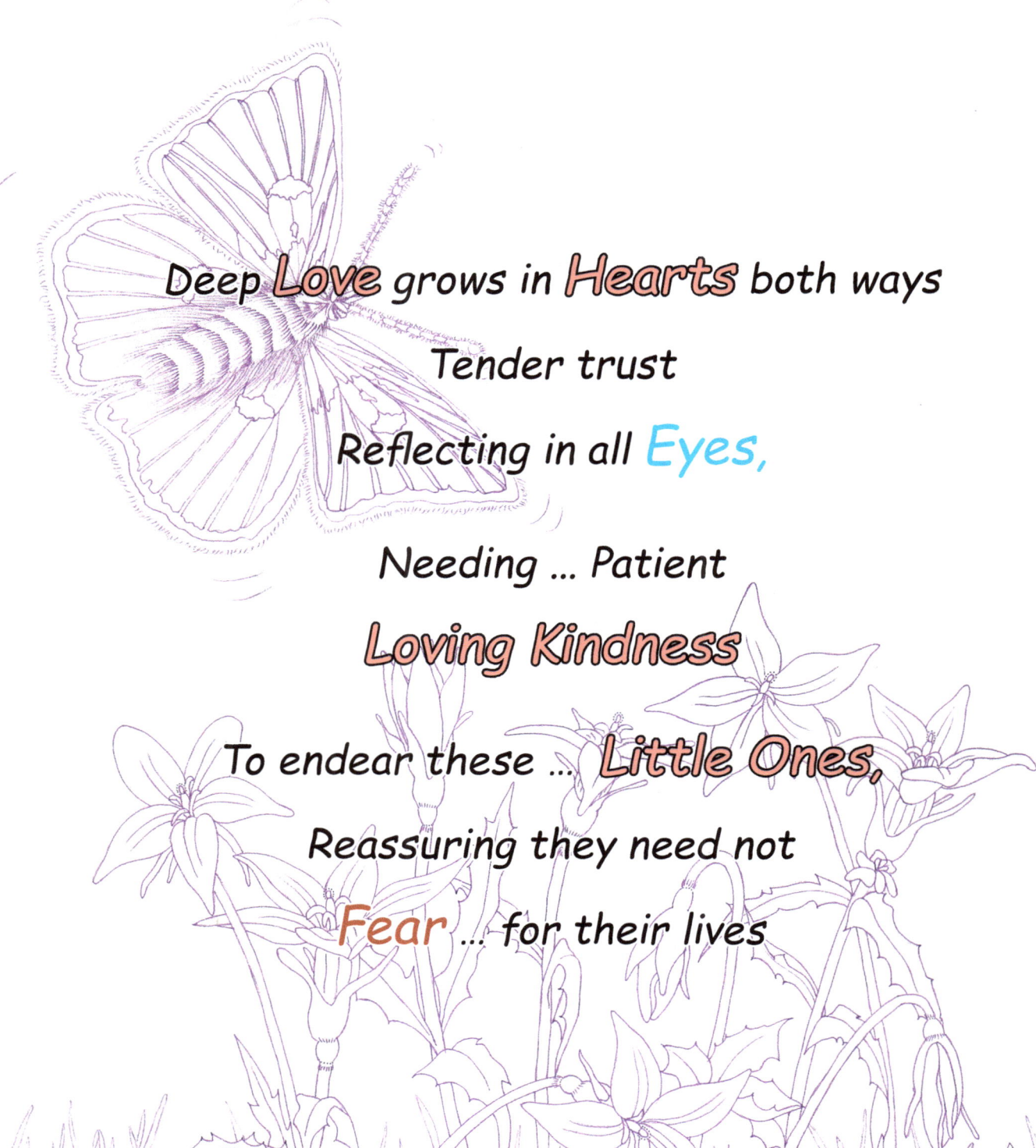

Deep *Love* grows in *Hearts* both ways

Tender trust

Reflecting in all *Eyes,*

Needing ... Patient

Loving Kindness

To endear these ... *Little Ones,*

Reassuring they need not

Fear ... for their lives

Two Hungry

Joeys

double feeding

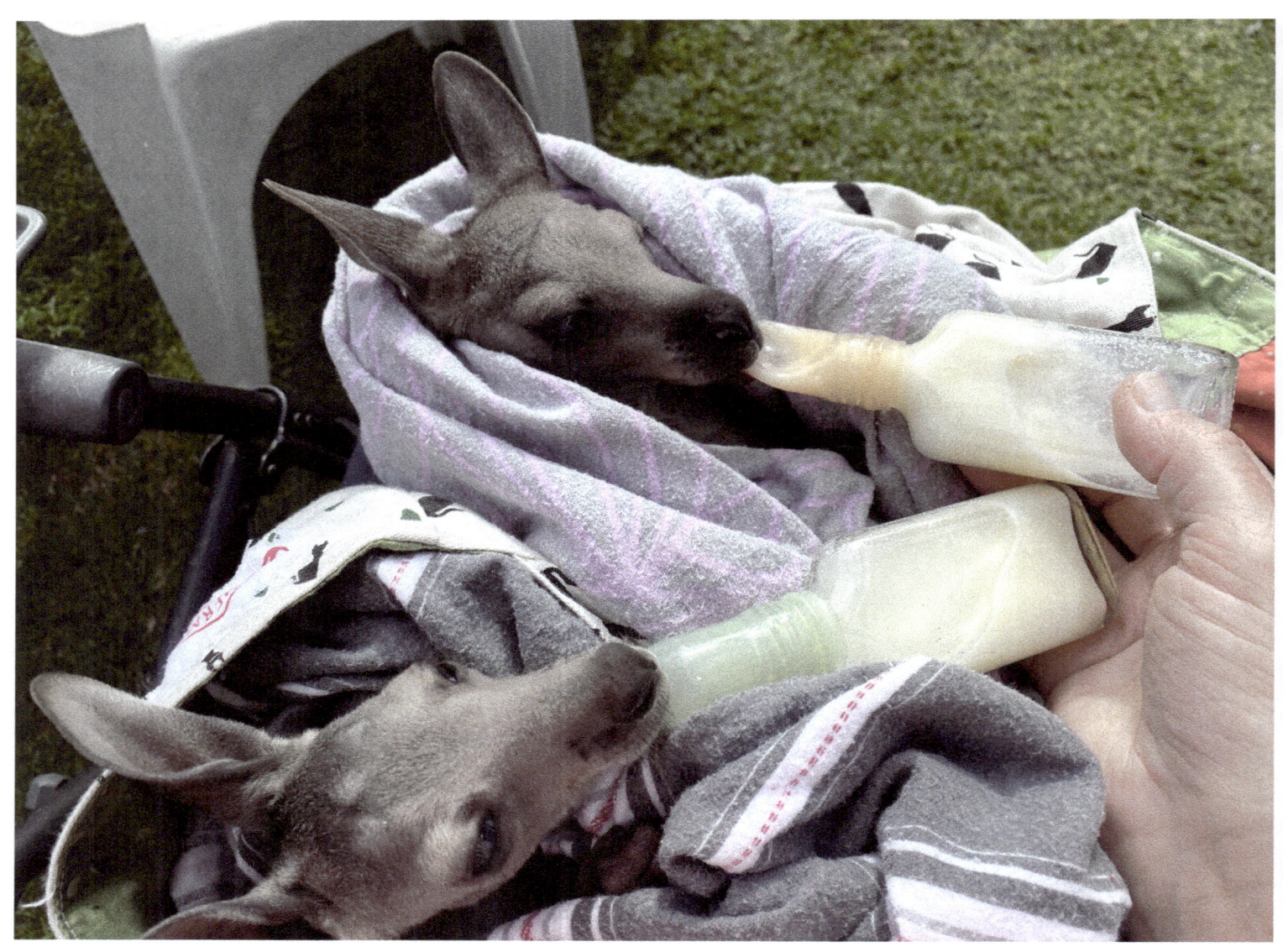

What ! A balancing ACT !

grabbing 'n pawing

for MORE !

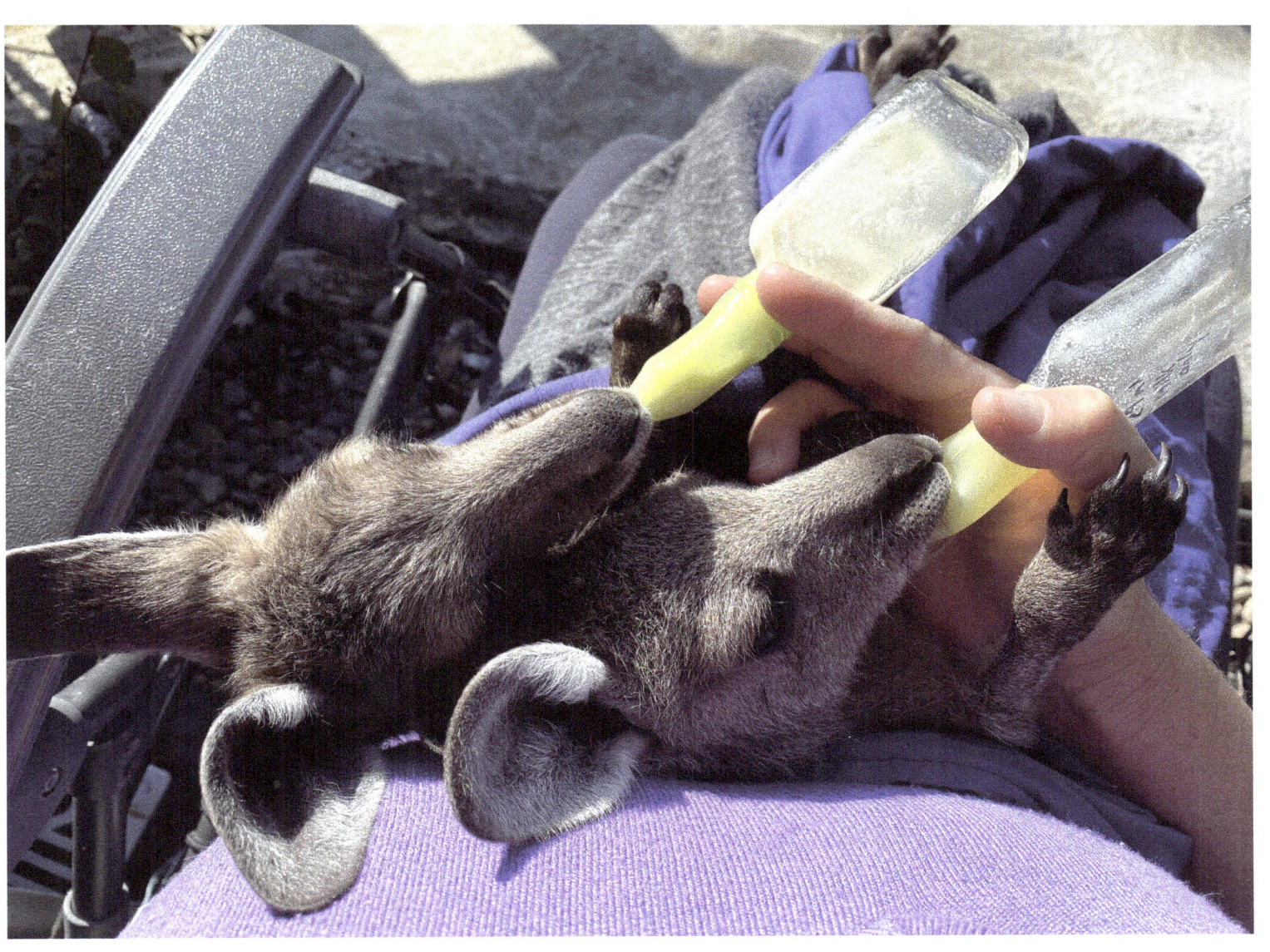

Mmmmmm ... milk coma

S l e e eeeepily snuggling

With a lil' snore

ZZZzzzzzzzzzzzzzzz

2 Brave little Peas attempting

'BOUNCey'S

awkwardly with ... BIG

Loooooooooooooong

feet,

WoBbLy ~ BoBbLy's

Burst's about ... Can little legs hold OUT!?

With a forward ... Roll 'n Tumble
safe again in a Bundle,

Snug 'n Sweet.

As little Joeys g r O W fur ... called

'Velvet' or

'Just Furring'

Start licking dirt ... when

heads hang L

O

W... to the ground,

It's the first of outside
YummiES ... to grow strong
tummiES

A healthy BOOST

with good ~ gut BUGS

... All round.

BB bites ... BIG ... dirt chunks

munching 'n chomping ... like snacking on

squishy ... LuMpS of mushy potatoes.

Sagey eats much less ... it's such a
sTiCkY mEsS

gritty's rollin' round ...

gUlping ... down it goes

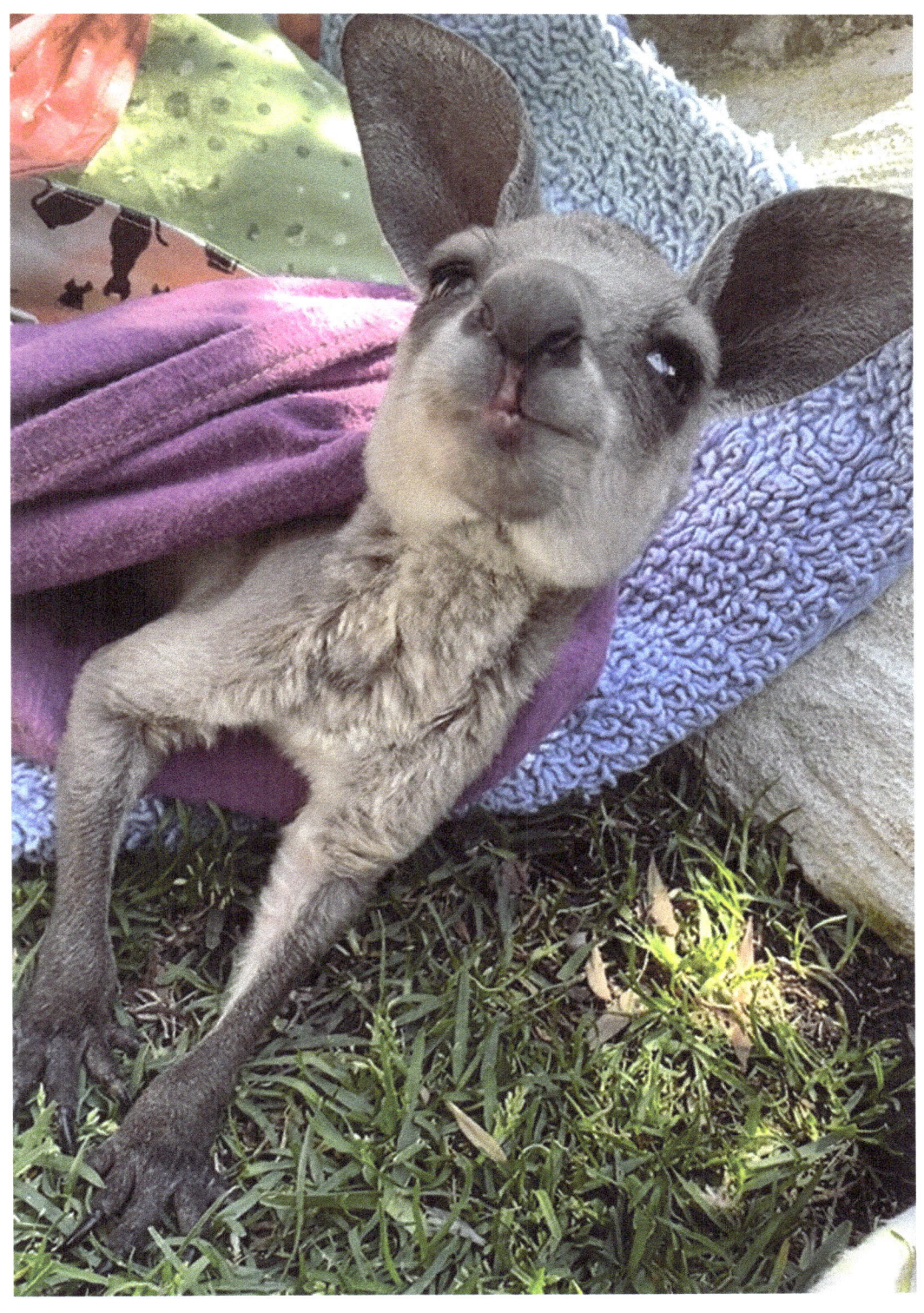

PLLLURRRRRK !

Sunny snuggling ... in pouch beds

'BB ... look who's home'

Yay ... it's Timby Wimby

excitedly ... Sagey nod's His head ~ 'Hello'

'G'day Lil' Matey' ... says Big Brother Timmy,

Nose to nose ... smell checking

With a 'tickle' from his hairy chinny

Kangaroos kiss this way ...
nuzzle 'n lick ~ nose to nose,

Sometimes bending low to the ground,

Sniff ... Shake ... Sniffing ~ Hello

Today's a bit scary ... bouncing in noisy car
Mumma up front steering

'*Mumma* ... is it very far?'

fresh crunchy ~ munchies

BB ... Peek-A-Booing ~ along the way,

Milk bottles ... Under BIG Shady Fig Tree,
Watching green hills ~ rolling away ...

Lush paddocks ... stretch out far ... beyond
Sight 'n Sea ...

'What Bouncey fun we could have,'
Sagey ... whispers to BB

discovering

All that's New ... while creating little

pathways along *Her* way

She's sooooo Funny

I must say ... Bluebelle in between plays

would climb in garden beds

Up HIGH !!!!!

For a little 'tinkle' ... a well stacked

Plop !

It's *Her* favourite ... little Spot, among

Flowers ~ Shrubs
where *She* could hide

Sagey Boi ' Boi ' ahhhhhh

Gently soft ... like the Herb,

FuZZy FuR 'n full of life

Eyes *Sparkling*

Questioning ... ???

' I ..... think ..... I ...... Can ???? '

' I .. THINK .. I .. Can ? '

' I THINK I JUST MIGHT ! '

So OFF 2 ~ **BIG** feet bound

a thrill 'n slight

WoBbLy ride,

Surprising even

Sagey Boi" Boi"

with a *'tingling'* ... Delight of

Pride !

Crisp Air ... Tingling ... 2 noses
with fresh ' BUSH ' cuttings,
A welcoming scent ... from where they
Belong.

Teasing ... tiny taste buds
with
Tantalising sensations ... mmmmm

Mouths attempt Rollin 'n Tossin ... Greens,

Nom!

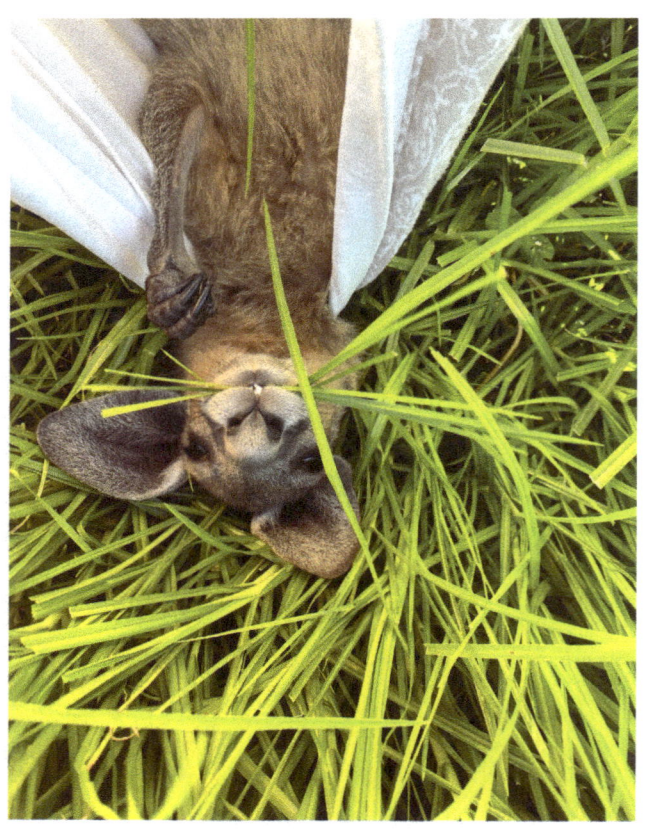

Nom!

Nom!

Burp!
'Oooooopsies ... pardon Me'

Swinging 'n
BipPity ~ BOpPing

... in swing pouches,

Like Mumma Roo ... would do,

Out for Nibbley's ... or just to Explore.

Chapter ~ 2

A Roo Resort'

Friends of BB 'n Sagey ~ Mumma too,
Hammer ~ cut ~ drill …
What a crew !

From a tin shed to … A building like no other … A Fancy … 'Cottage' … sort,

'A Roo Resort'

Wow ... 5 months in the build ...

Hop ... Hop ... Hooray!

A Grand Opening ~ The Greatest Thrill

Swing pouch snuggling ~ with a garden view

For many months ... heavy rains fell ...

Yard becomes a water well ...

with little rivers passing by ...

'Cottage' snuggles BB 'n Sagey ~ warm 'n dry

65

BB learns stand ~ feeding ... during the rain,

Yay ~ *Sun's shining* again ...

'Look Mumma ~ it's like driving a car

sssssslurp ... sssssslurp

just not moving very far'

Sagey eager ... tail 'n feet balancing,

paws hold tight too ...

'Here goes tummy ~ mmmmm ...

Warm delicious ~ yummy'

'See Mumma … I can do it like BB'
Sagey's fluffy chest … feeling proud ~ indeed !

There were days ... BB and

Sagey ... Came D

                              O

                              W

                              N

... Unwell too,

YucKiEs making them

'S H A K Y ~ W E A K'

even blue

Ohhhhhhh ...Worrying times indeed ... Quiet rest A Vital neeeeeed, gentle care, extra bottles 'n snuggles ... would get them through.

Helping to recover
'Cottage' ... Safely cradles
Bubba ~ Lubba's
with the
BIGGEST
Bouquet 'n Yummiest ... Bite !

Fresh ... She Oak
...Westringia
... Bottlebrush 'n Banksia

Varieties of Bark
Handfuls of Hay ... sliced,

A Delicious Plate of dirt,

Basket ... spilling grass ... like a skirt

Yummies ... Ready for a Party * on a * Moonlit night. *

Morning hurry's in ...

Refreshing Light * *... with* **BB** *Super Bright,*

Eagerly waiting at

'Cottage' door !

Early
Sunrays ... *Glisten*
on Dew Drops
Across the Garden Floor

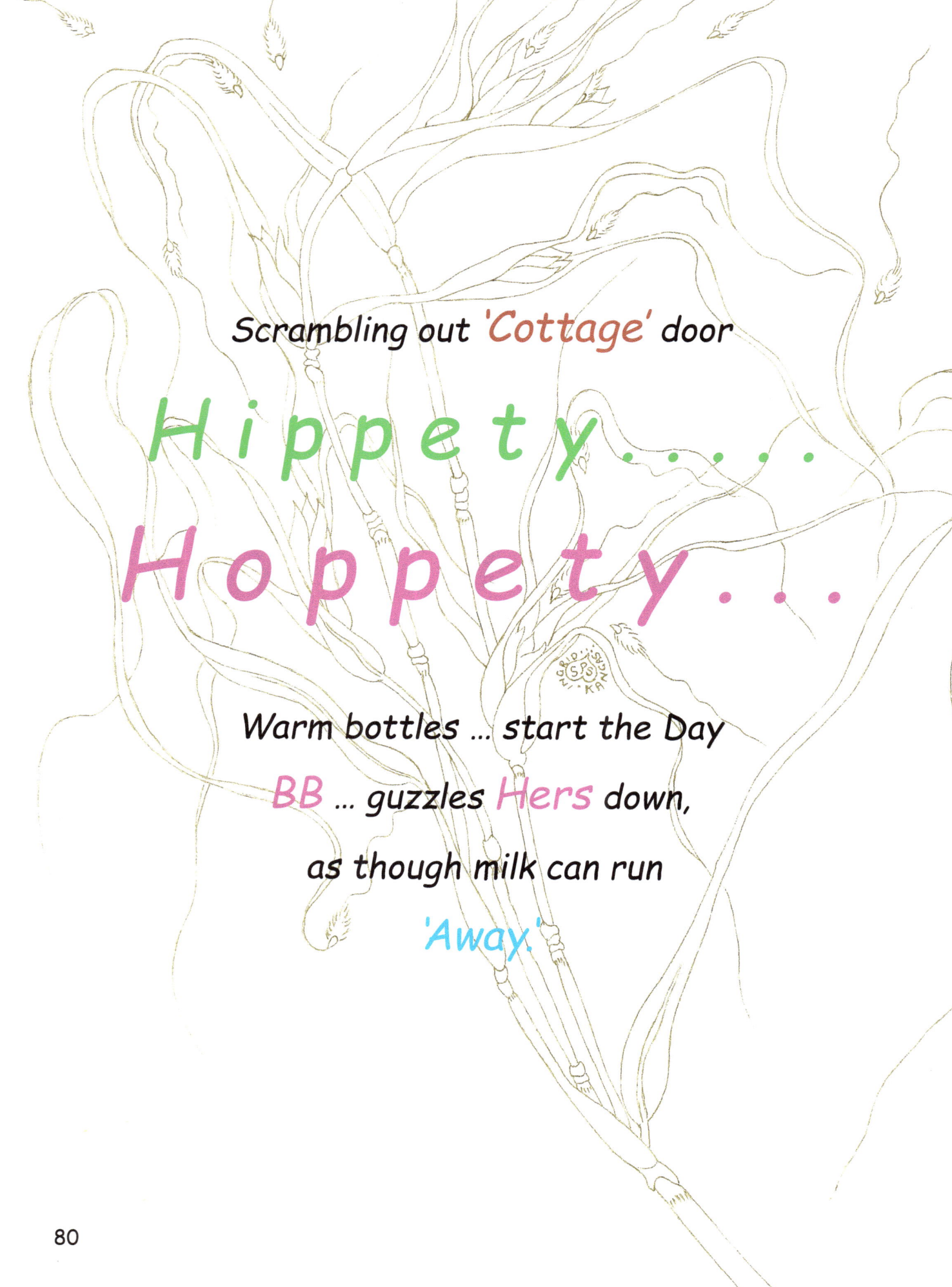

Scrambling out 'Cottage' door

Hippety....

Hoppety...

Warm bottles ... start the Day

BB ... guzzles Hers down,

as though milk can run

'Away.'

Sagey ... gently takes
His time,
Two paws
lightly placed so ... fine
upon *My* knee,

while wrapped ... sooooooo
Tightly ... *My* finger is
with **BB's** ... paw.

Bubba ~ Lubba's ... PARTY

through Dark night ... unseen,

Soooooooooooooo

'Cottage' ... Needs a

Brilliant clean !

Whhhhhaaaat ... a Mess !!!

' Tinkles ' marking

B I G W ET Spots,

Wall to Wall ... Of ...

Plop !   Plop !   Plops !

Dirt ... Bark ... Scattered YuMMieS ... such busy little tuMMieS, creating a ...

wOWZER

... Of a scene ...

That's for sure !

'Cottage' Sparkling for Bubba ~ Lubba's ... once more

' BB ... I think ... Mumma's snoring ?

Let's Messy Fun with 'Tinkle' spots 'n

Plop ! Plop ! Galoring '

Now there's gardening to do ...

BB ... Sagey Helping too ...

Trimming grass

is what They Do sooooo

Super ... well,

Clipping ... pulling weeds

Birds chirping ... Buzzing Bees,

Sagey hiding while ...

BB's ... discovering a
Flowers ~ Smell.

BB ~ Alert ! ... to any Sounds ! Changes ! Movements !

SUDDENLY
near by

Her ears ... attentively

UP ... STRAIGHT

Listening,

PAWS PULLED

to *Her* chest

HIGH !

'Who's there …?'

It's … Big John B

'Come 'n Play ~ There's No Rules'

Sagey Boi ' Boi ' … loves …

' HOP '

' Bounce ' ... ' Kicking ! '

'Oooooooch !'

It's safe to say ... He's quite little,

Yet sooo ... BIG 'n Brave !

You see ... little Joeys ... first try this

with trusting ~ Mumma Roos,

Growing them ready for the

Wild 'n Protecting them too !

After Plays ... there's a time of Day

where Roos ... like

Napping ... for a

Pouchy sway ... or

A
Looooooooooooooooooooooong
... stretch Out ...!

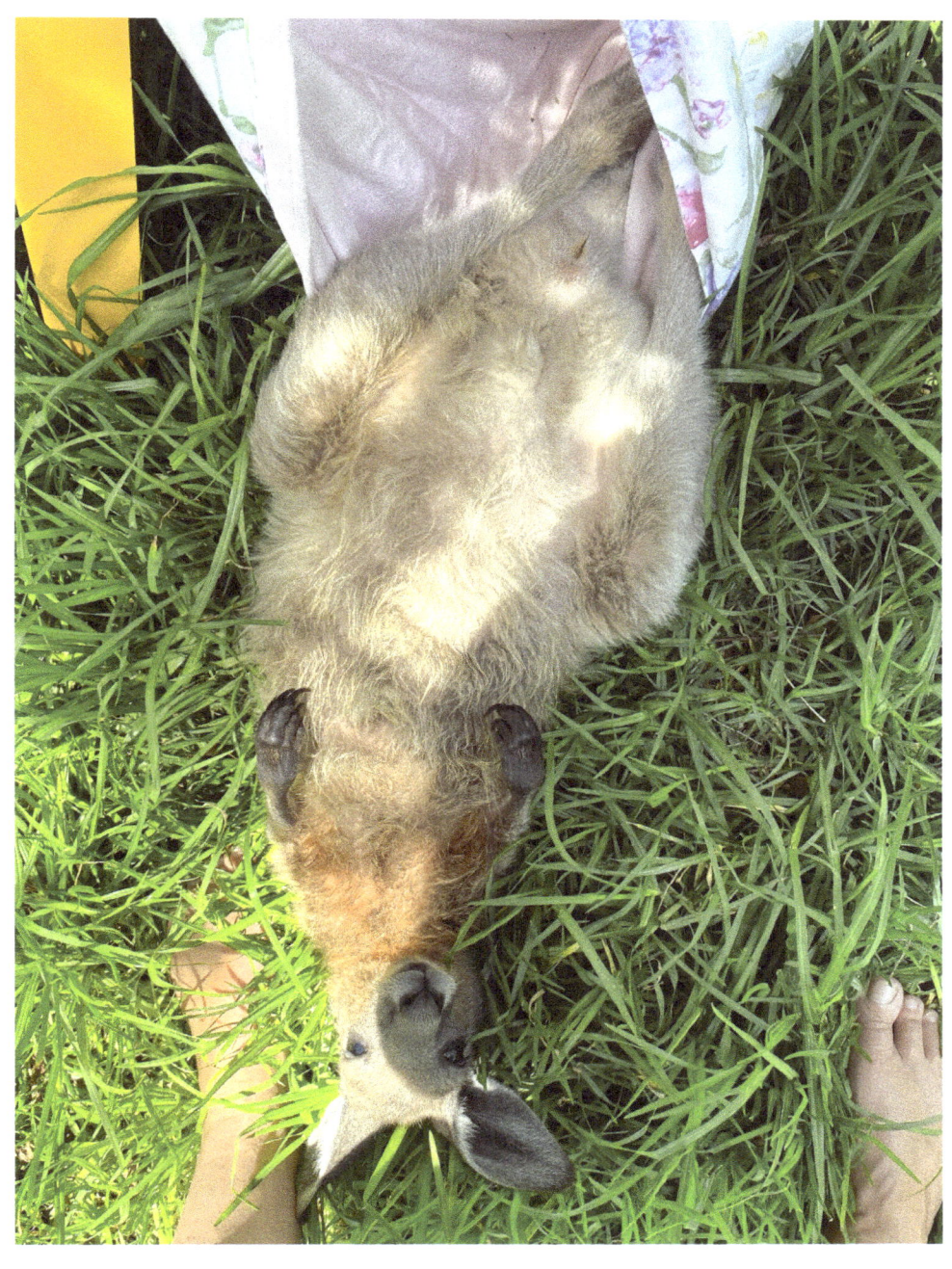

Sagey's wise ... Heading

to their 'Cottage'

It's HOT ! ... Outside ...

snoooooooozie's

zzzzzzzzzzzz

Not for roaming about !

Afternoon shadows stretch ~ in fading light

Sagey's snuggling ...
BB's watching ...
Sun's disappearing ... sight

Nighty *Night*

Bluebelle & Sagey Boi ' Boi '

To Be Continued ~ '
A Diary of Two Orphaned Joeys ~ book 2'

' Two … Sweet … Bounceeey … Feet '

This story is written, photographed,
video graphed from true events
July 2021 ~ July 2022
By Ingrid Lorraine Kangas

In Loving Kindness
Fully Trained Carer ~ Under a Registered ~
Licensed Wildlife Group

Thank You for purchasing this Story ~
every book purchased ~ gifts a percentage of sales,
donated to ~ Registered Carers, Rehabilitation
Clinics & Sanctuaries, to help support the care of
orphaned or injured Kangaroos

Acknowledgements ~ Thank you dearly

~ Michael S, John B, Timothy G for helping Me to build 'Roo Resort Cottage'
~ Akiko, John B, Michael S in helping to support Me in the care of BB & Sagey,
Lynnette S ~ making amazing pouches,
Mel L ~ helping with technical work for this book,
John B ~ for your encouraging support with this book 'n giggles along the way.

Amazing Wildlife Carers across Australia ~ as we work & learn together, we achieve so much more for Our Magnificent Kangaroos ~ Wildlife

About the Author ~ Illustrator, Ingrid Lorraine Kangas,

Born in Sydney & raised on the beautiful South Coast, NSW

1972 ~ 2001
& also in the Latrobe Region, Vic

1977 ~ 1981
My deep love of nature, its amazing designs, colours, creatures, fascinates, inspires and delights me always, since such a young age, storytelling ~ illustrating has always been one of my passions

I feel very strongly about saving & protecting Our Magnificent Kangaroos, Along with All Our Precious Wildlife and Their Habitats.

I feel very honoured when I am able to help Our Amazing Wildlife
~ Every Life Matters
~ We Are All Connected

~ How We Treat Life Around Us
Has A Rippling Effect

~ I continue to train & learn always for the loving, gentle, care Our Wildlife Deserves

~ Thank you to those who handle with loving, gentle, respect, knowing that Wildlife

~ feel pain

~ feel emotion

~ Always contact Your Local Wildlife Group, so that injured or orphaned Wildlife can be placed with a trained Carer.

www.ingramcontent.com/pod-product-compliance
Lightning Source LLC
Chambersburg PA
CBHW051316110526
44590CB00031B/4373